12/25/18

Dear Nik,

Son, you have brought so much happiness to my life. The love and joy and pride I feel because of you give me rewards that cannot be measured. Thank you for the bright light that shines through as you. I love you!

You are my everything!

ma

Titles by Marci
Published by
Blue Mountain Arts®

Angels Are Everywhere!
Angels Bring a Message
of Hope Whenever It Is Needed

Friends Are Forever
A Gift of Inspirational Thoughts
to Thank You for Being
My Friend

10 Simple Things to Remember
An Inspiring Guide to
Understanding Life

To My Granddaughter
A Gift of Love and Wisdom
to Always Carry
in Your Heart

To My Mother
I Will Always Carry
Your Love in My Heart

To My Sister
A Gift of Love and Inspiration
to Thank You
for Being My Sister

To My Son
Love and Encouragement
to Carry with You on Your
Journey Through Life

You Are My "Once in a Lifetime"
I Will Always Love You

To My Son

Love and Encouragement
to Carry with you on your
Journey Through Life

Marci

Blue Mountain Press™
Boulder, Colorado

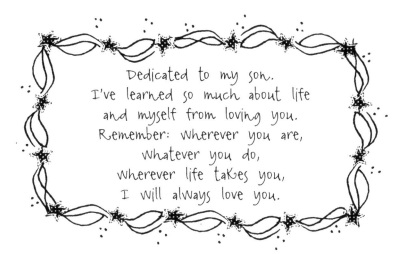

Dedicated to my son.
I've learned so much about life
and myself from loving you.
Remember: wherever you are,
whatever you do,
wherever life takes you,
I will always love you.

Library of Congress Control Number: 2014957957
ISBN: 978-1-59842-866-7

Children of the Inner Light is a registered trademark. Used under license.
Certain trademarks are used under license.

Printed in China.
Third Printing: 2016

 This book is printed on recycled paper.

This book is printed on paper that has been specially produced to be acid free (neutral pH) and contains no groundwood or unbleached pulp. It conforms with the requirements of the American National Standards Institute, Inc., so as to ensure that this book will last and be enjoyed by future generations.

Blue Mountain Arts, Inc.
P.O. Box 4549, Boulder, Colorado 80306

Contents

Son, your birth was a joy and a blessing! Having you in my life has provided me with my greatest opportunity for growth, and for that I am grateful. Watching you grow and develop has provided me with some of my greatest joys. Watching you learn from your journey has taught me how to let go. Your talents and potential are extraordinary, and I give thanks for the gift of being your parent.

From the
Very Beginning...

We Have Had
a Special
Connection

The day you came into my life was a beautiful day for me. Like an answered prayer, you were placed in my arms, and I knew we had made a connection. Loving you has allowed me to experience unconditional love. Seeing you pursue your dreams has given me inspiration. Sharing your happiness has taught me the meaning of joy. Your love will always be in my heart and mine in yours. The bond we have found is as everlasting as the spirit.

Dear
Son...

You Changed
My Life
for the Better

Being a parent has changed my life in ways that are hard to describe. The love I feel for you is stronger than I ever dreamed possible, and the sense of responsibility is larger than I ever imagined. When I look at you, I see the future about to unfold. I want so much for you to find your place in the world... to understand the meaning of love... to know the satisfaction found in relationships. I was touched by God's hand when He gave you to me as my son.

You Are a

Shining Star

Some people have a special light around them from the day they are born... It shines brightly and makes them stand out in a crowd. You are one of those people! Your heart is always open, ready to share or just listen to those in need. Your arms are always ready with a hug and a reminder that God has a plan. Thank you for the inspiration you are and for the bright light that shines as you. You are a shining star!

Never Forget

You Are Loved

♥

Never forget and never doubt how much you are loved. As surely as the sun rises each morning... and with the same certainty that the moon will affect the tides... Know that I will always love you with all my heart.

♥

♥

Please
Remember
This, Son...

The Road of Life
Has Many Turns

Sometimes the road of life will take you to a place you had planned... Sometimes it will show you a surprise around the bend you could never have anticipated. You must make decisions based on the information you have... accept the ups and downs as they come... and live "one day at a time." Often you will find it is only when you look back that you can see that what you had thought was a "wrong turn" was a right one after all!

Here Is Some Wisdom for Your Journey...

as you Follow Life's Path

No matter where life takes you or what path you choose, you will always meet challenges... that is the way life is. There are no guarantees, and no matter how many things you do right or how many rules you follow, there will always be that fork in the road that makes you choose between this way or that. Whenever you meet this place, remember these things: You are loved... love will sustain you. You are strong... prayer will get you through anything. You are wise... the greatest gift of all lies within you.

10 Simple Things to Remember

1. Love is why we are here.

2. The most important day is today.

3. If you always do your best, you will not have regrets.

4. In spite of your best efforts, some things are just out of your control.

5. Things will always look better tomorrow.

6. Sometimes a wrong turn will bring you to exactly the right place.

7. Sometimes when you think the answer is "no," it is just "not yet."

8. True friends share your joy, see the best in you, and support you through your challenges.

9. God and your parents will always love you.

10. For all your accomplishments, nothing will bring you more happiness than the love you find.

A Son's Love

Is Forever

A son is a gift of hopes and dreams wrapped up in a beautiful life.

A son is an opportunity to reflect upon the past and a chance to see possibilities fulfilled.

A son carries hopes from the past and dreams of the future in his heart...

A son's path is his to walk;
a son's dreams are his to create;
a son's happiness is his to define.

A son is understanding, Kind,
compassionate, caring, and giving.

A son reminds you of how much
you are loved.

A son is a precious gift that is unwrapped a little bit each year.

A son shares the journey of life, celebrating love and joy and tears and hopes as only a son can.

A son's love remains forever in your heart.

The Bond
Between Us

Is Everlasting

From the first moment I laid eyes on you, we made a connection. You have brought a love and joy to my life that only a parent could know. I watched you grow and have come to understand that our lives have been brought together for a reason. I have learned as much from you as you have from me. Thank you for your love and for sharing all that is uniquely you. The bond we have found is everlasting.

I always wanted a son... someone to share wisdom and hope with... someone to love and encourage through life's challenges... someone to be proud of, as I watched dreams be fulfilled and wishes come true. What a wonderful feeling to know I have what I always wanted... in you!

The Story of Your Birth

Is a Story of Joy

So often, I look back and think about the day you were born. There was so much joy at the news that you were on the way and so much anticipation about what the future would bring. Hopes and dreams were formed... love was strong... our hearts were open and ready.

I had a sense before you were born that you already knew who you were... I was so right! you came into the world with a strong spirit ready to learn... a kind heart ready to give... and a gentle soul ready to love. No child has ever been loved or wanted more.

These Are the Things I Wish for You

I wish you a life filled with love... a true love to share your every dream... family love to warm your heart... and priceless love found in the gift of friendship.

I wish you peace... peace in
knowing who you are... peace in
knowing what you believe in... and
peace in the understanding of what
is important in life.

I wish you joy... joy as you awaken
each day with gratitude in your
heart for new beginnings... joy
when you take in the power of a
mighty storm and allow it to fill you
with courage... and joy, a hundred
times returned, for each time you've
brought happiness to another's heart.

Remember I am thinking of you...
believing in you... praying for you... and
hoping you know that no matter how
big a problem seems or how hopeless you
feel, you are never alone, as God's grace
is only one request away!

Hope Is
a Gift

Hope

Hope is believing that
miracles are possible!

We Give
to Ourselves

Oftentimes our path seems to be filled with roadblocks, and we wonder why life is so difficult. Things happen that leave us feeling as though we have little control over our circumstances. Remember that hope is a gift we can give to ourselves... When we choose this attitude and tap into our inner reserves, we are rewarded with the knowledge of what we have learned in life. The decision to look forward, stay positive, and remain hopeful is a key that unlocks the door to possibilities, and, when shared, returns to renew the spirit. May the power of hope be with you every day.

Listen for that voice inside guiding you toward the right thing to do, the right path to travel, and the knowledge of what will bring you happiness and fulfillment. That voice is very quiet, like a whisper. Over time, and mostly through the challenges in life, you will learn to hear it more clearly. Whenever you feel that tug to do something new, help someone in need, or share what you have learned, listen carefully... and follow your heart toward your dreams.

5 Keys
to Happiness

1. Realize that happiness is a choice... you can make the decision to "be happy" each day.

2. Remember that happiness is contagious. Make someone smile, and the good feelings come right back to you.

3. Be grateful for the little things in life that are free. Make a list, and add to it each morning.

4. Believe that ultimately everything happens for a reason. Acceptance leads the way to happiness.

5. Give away some courage every day! When you encourage another to "keep going," "hang in there," or "believe in their dreams," you will find an unending source of happiness.

Hold On to Family...

Family

Time Spent With Loved Ones Creates an Everlasting Bond

Families are special creations made up of people who love one another and are tied together with threads of common experience, memories, and values. You are such a special part of our family and a gift to me every day.

Hold On
to Friends...

Time Spent
With Friends
Creates Lifelong
Sweet Memories

Friendship is one of life's greatest treasures, and it is a gift that lasts a lifetime. We create bonds during times in our lives when our beliefs and our experiences are shaping who we are. Those bonds cannot be broken by the passing of time, even when life gets so busy that we lose touch. Let friends know that you think of them often... and they will always have a special place in your heart.

Hold On
to Your Dreams...

Because Anything
Is Possible

Your life holds for you endless possibilities. You have built a solid foundation, and you have worked hard for it. Continue to do what is necessary to move forward one day at a time. Write down your dream and tuck it away — entrusting that all things will come at the right time. Keep sight always of what is important in life.

Remember that true happiness and purpose will be found in relationships — in the workplace and at home. Live each day open to guidance, and your purpose will be revealed to you...

Remember that you are special. There are talents locked away inside you just waiting for the right time to unfold.

Remember that dreams are the start of every great adventure. When you close your eyes and imagine your happy and successful self in the future, you are beginning your journey!

Remember to listen to your heart...
it is where your courage lies. When
you follow your heart, you may meet
challenges, but each of your steps will
be guided.

Remember that "today" is always the
most important day. Enjoy every
moment of it, and may your dreams
come true!

Hold hands with the one you love, no matter how old you are. Say "I love you" every day. Write love notes for your special someone to find. Forget mistakes. Forgive words spoken too soon. Plan time alone together. Focus on the things you like about each other. Do not expect perfection. Try to be the person of your dreams. Support each other through life's challenges. Say "thank you"... everyone needs to be appreciated. Send e-mails that say "I love you." Take walks together. Hug and kiss every day.

When Good
Things Come into
Your Life...

Pass Them On!

We each have a chance to brighten the day of another. It can be a kind smile... a simple hello... shared inspiration... or an unexpected gesture to let someone know that their being in the world makes a difference. When good things come into your life, I hope you'll be inspired to brighten the day of another. Pass them on!

You Can
Make a
Difference...

Let Your Light
Shine!

Live your beliefs... and be a powerful example of love in the world.

Be compassionate... Life is difficult, and people are often working through private battles.

Demonstrate acts of kindness... "Little ones" are watching you and learning about compassion.

Encourage someone today... The words "everything will be okay" can lighten the heart of another.

Share love... There is an endless supply.

Be hopeful... Your attitude will uplift the spirit of another.

May you
Be Blessed
with...

Faith, Hope,
and Love

May you be blessed with all the good things in life... faith, hope, love, and the blessing of good friends. If you have these things, whatever challenges life brings, you will get through. Your faith will light your path... hope will keep you strong... the love you give to others will bring you joy... and your friendships will remind you of what is important in life.

When you need encouragement, remember these things:

You are stronger than you realize.

Life's inevitable adversities call forth our courage.

You have a lot of wisdom inside you.

God's plan will unfold with perfect timing.

The voice of your soul will lead the way.

A hug from my heart is only a phone call away!

When you were just a song in my heart, I wanted you... when you were just a babe in my womb, I loved you... when you were only one day old, I knew my life had changed forever. Thank you for your love that brightens my life and for the "gift of you" that makes me so proud. The love and joy and pride I feel because you are my son give me rewards that cannot be measured.

I'm So Glad
You Are My Child

When I became a parent, I expected to love you... I wasn't prepared to experience love in a whole new way that I never knew existed!

When I became a parent, I expected to care about your well-being... I found that caring for you became the most important thing in my life.

When I became a parent, I thought I knew all about life... but you taught me about a whole new world — a world where hopes and dreams were new... where the sacrifices of parenthood called me to be more than I ever thought I could be... and where I experienced a connection that allowed me to understand the purpose of life. I am so glad you are my child.

"I love you," and I want you to always remember what you mean to me. The joys we have shared and the memories we have made through our lives are a gift beyond measure. Thank you for your love. Today, consider yourself hugged!

I say a prayer for you every day
and ask your guardian angel to
stay by your side... to bring you
inspiration when life gets you down...
to fill your heart with determination
when life puts obstacles in your
path... and to shower you with grace
to nurture your spiritual growth as
you travel your path through life.
May your angel wrap you in God's
love every day!

Son, These Are My Promises to You

I promise...

To always love you...

To always see your beautiful soul shining through...

To support you in finding your talents...

To encourage you always to do your best...

To listen when you need to talk...

To remind you by example of what is important in life...

To give you support when you make mistakes...

To celebrate your accomplishments and give hope to your dreams...

To take the "journey of life" with you... sharing birthdays and holidays, triumphs and sadness, the good and the bad, today and tomorrow, and all of the things that bind us together forever.

There are times in our lives when our inner struggles are so great that we can't really express how we feel. These are the times when we need to know that someone is there for us, that someone cares about what is best for us, and that someone loves us no matter what. Remember, I am always here for you... I will always love you... and I'll stand by you, no matter how hard life gets.

When we have worked so hard and given so much of ourselves, we wonder about the "why of it all" when things don't go as planned. Remember that timing is important. There is a right time for everything, and the universe will unfold its magnificent plan in a time that is not ours to decide. We must have faith that a power greater than ourselves knows what is best for us... and when. It is often only when we look back at the path behind us that we realize the perfect timing in which our dreams have come true.

Something
to Remember
Every Day...

Keep It Simple

Keep life simple.

Believe that everything is working out for your highest good.

Live each day one at a time.

Let go of things you cannot change.

Have faith... your angel is always with you, enfolding you in God's grace.

Know that you are loved.

Thank You
for Sharing

Your Beautiful Spirit
with Me

When I became a parent, I expected to become a teacher, as I believed it was my job to guide you through life. I have found, though, that I have been given a wonderful gift, as I have had the opportunity to learn about unconditional love. I have learned to "let go" and trust you to find your way. Thank you for that opportunity and for sharing your beautiful spirit with me.

Wasn't it just yesterday that you were a baby in my arms? I looked at your precious face and wondered where life would take you. Today, I look at the person you've become... strong, kind, thoughtful, caring, and optimistic, and I realize that the dreams I held in my heart for you are alive in you.

Son,
You Have Given Me
So Many Wonderful
Memories

We receive many gifts throughout our lives, and in time, we realize that the most precious gifts are the tiny, special moments that live in our hearts and make us who we are. You have given me so many of those memories to save.

I was there to hear your first heartbeat... I was there to watch you take your first steps... I saw you develop friendships, learn from mistakes, and grab on to independence... I am so grateful to be watching and sharing your journey.

I
Love You

...and I
Believe in You

There have never been words
more powerful than
"I love you"...
or more meaningful than
"Thank you"...
or more sustaining than
"I believe in you"...
So I'm saying these things to you now:
"I love you more than words can say.
I am so thankful you are a part of my life.
And no matter what,
I will always believe in you!"

You are always in my prayers, and I want you to remember that so you will be open to the grace that comes your way. I have asked that you feel the love of God like a gentle breeze when you need inspiration... that your faith remain unwavering through all of life's challenges... and that hope be the burning light that always guides your way.

My Son,
I wish you a life that is now and forever blessed with these important gifts:

* Faith to guide your path.

* Comfort in times of uncertainty.

* Friendship always surrounding you.

* Hope in every situation.

* Acceptance of your losses.

* Understanding that your greatest gifts are the things that are free.

* Joy in all you do.

* Peace to soothe your soul.

* Courage to be yourself.

* Dreams never-ending.

* Love always in your heart.

When I look at you and how you've grown, I feel so proud. It's not just your physical presence but your shining spirit that lights up my world! I don't know where the time has gone... or when yesterday became today... but each time I think of the joy you are in my life, all that comes to mind is "you are amazing!"

My Son,
My Child,
My Heart...

My Love Is Always
With You

You are always in my heart and never far from my thoughts, because on the day you were born, I promised to love you forever. My wish is that you find a place in the world that gives you a sense of contribution... that you find the kind of love that makes the stars shine brighter... and that you know the gift of gratitude that comes with living a life of compassion. Remember, wherever you are, whatever you do, wherever life takes you, I will always love you.

About Marci

Marci began her career by hand painting floral designs on clothing. No one was more surprised than she was when one day, in a single burst of inspiration and a completely new and different art style, her delightful characters sprang from her pen! "Their wild and crazy hair is a sign of strength," she thought, "and their crooked little smiles are endearing." She quickly identified the charming characters as Mother, Daughter, Sister, Father, Son, Friend, and so on until all the people and places in life were filled. Then, with her own loved ones in mind, she wrote a true and special sentiment to each one. This would be the beginning of a wonderful success story, which today still finds Marci writing each and every one of her verses in this same personal way.

Marci is a self-taught artist who has always enjoyed writing and art. She is thrilled to see how her delightful characters and universal messages of love have touched the hearts and lives of people everywhere. Her distinctive designs can also be found on Blue Mountain Arts greeting cards, calendars, bookmarks, and other gift items.

To learn more about Marci, look for Children of the Inner Light on Facebook or visit her website: WWW.MARCIonline.com.